**NATIONAL
GEOGRAPHIC**

Greenland's Ocean Region

USING EARTH'S RESOURCES

Moana Ashley

PICTURE CREDITS
Cover: iceberg in Disko Bay, Greenland © Tom Stewart/Corbis/
Tranz; boats by harbor, icebergs in water, Greenland © Peter Tyson/
photolibrary.com.

page 1 © Tom Stewart/Corbis/Tranz; page 4 (bottom left) © Wayne
Lawler; Ecoscene/Corbis/Tranz; page 4 (bottom right) © Wolfgang
Kaehler/Corbis/Tranz; page 5 (top) © Peter Guttman/Corbis/
Tranz; page 5 (bottom left), Photodisc; page 5 (bottom right) © Jim
Zuckerman/Corbis/Tranz; page 6 © Hubert Stadler/Corbis/Tranz;
page 8 © Robert van der Hilst/Corbis/Tranz; page 11 © Wolfgang
Kaehler/Corbis/Tranz; page 12 (top) © Peter Reynolds/Frank Lane
Picture Agency/Corbis/Tranz; page 12 (bottom) © Kim Sayer/Corbis/
Tranz; page 13 © Charles & Josette Lenars/Corbis/Tranz;
page 15 © Torleif Svensson/Corbis/Tranz; page 16 © Jose Luis
Pelaez, Inc./Corbis/Tranz; page 21 © Tom Stewart/Corbis/Tranz;
page 22 © Staffan Widstrand/Corbis/Tranz; page 23 © Roy Corral/
Corbis/Tranz; page 24, the signing of the Stockholm Convention
© courtesy of Earth Negotiations Bulletin/ IISD; page 26 © Galen
Rowell/Corbis/Tranz; page 29, Brand X Pictures.

Produced through the worldwide resources of the National Geographic
Society, John M. Fahey, Jr., President and Chief Executive Officer;
Gilbert M. Grosvenor, Chairman of the Board; Nina D. Hoffman,
Executive Vice President and President, Books and Education
Publishing Group.

PREPARED BY NATIONAL GEOGRAPHIC SCHOOL PUBLISHING
Ericka Markman, Senior Vice President and President, Children's
Books and Education Publishing Group; Steve Mico, Vice President and
Editorial Director; Marianne Hiland, Executive Editor; Richard Easby,
Editorial Manager; Jim Hiscott, Design Manager; Kristin Hanneman,
Illustrations Manager; Matt Wascavage, Manager of Publishing
Services; Sean Philpotts, Production Manager.

EDITORIAL MANAGEMENT
Morrison BookWorks, LLC

PROGRAM CONSULTANTS
Dr. Shirley V. Dickson, Program Director, Literacy, Education
Commission of the States; James A. Shymansky, E. Desmond Lee
Professor of Science Education, University of Missouri-St. Louis.

National Geographic Theme Sets program developed by Macmillan
Science and Education Australia Pty Limited.

Published by the National Geographic Society
1145 17th Street, N.W.
Washington, D.C. 20036-4688

ISBN: 978-0-7922-4763-0
ISBN: 0-7922-4763-9

Printed in China by The Central Printing (Hong Kong) Ltd.
Quarry Bay, Hong Kong
Supplier Code: OCP May 2018
Macmillan Job: 804263
Cengage US PO: 15308030

MEA10_May18_S

Contents

Using Earth's Resources

Nature provides people with many useful things. Air, water, plants, animals, minerals, and fuels all come from nature. Things that come from nature are called natural resources. Natural resources are found everywhere on Earth. They are found in the rain forests of Indonesia, the ocean region of Greenland, the deserts of Australia, and the mountains of Peru.

 ## Key Concepts..

1. Earth provides many natural resources that people can use.
2. Different resources are useful to people in different ways.
3. Conservation and recycling can help save resources.

Four Resource-Rich Regions

Tropical Rain Forests

The trees in Indonesia's rain forests have many important uses.

Oceans

The oceans around Greenland teem with marine animals.

In this book you will learn about the resources found in Greenland's ocean region.

GR 15-117

Deserts

The deserts of Australia provide people with fuels and minerals.

Mountains

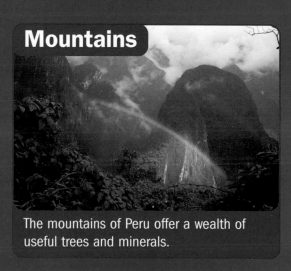

The mountains of Peru offer a wealth of useful trees and minerals.

Ocean Resources

Imagine a place where ocean waters are so cold that ice drifts on the surface. The waters around Greenland are like this. If you think such waters would be too cold for animals, you may be surprised. Beneath the surface, the waters around Greenland teem with life. Few other places in the world are home to so many ocean animals.

The World's Oceans

Oceans cover 71 percent of Earth's surface. Oceans are home to fish and other **marine** animals. Marine animals are animals that spend time in ocean waters. People all over the world use marine animals for food and other products. The oceans have an effect on Earth's climate as well.

Icy ocean near Greenland

The Ocean Region of Greenland

Greenland is a country surrounded by ocean. It is the world's largest island. Greenland lies northeast of Canada, between the Arctic and North Atlantic Oceans. Most of Greenland is covered by a thick layer of ice all year round. Crops are hard to grow in the cold climate. People mostly fish and hunt for food instead. Most people in Greenland live along the coast.

Look at the map to see the location of Greenland.

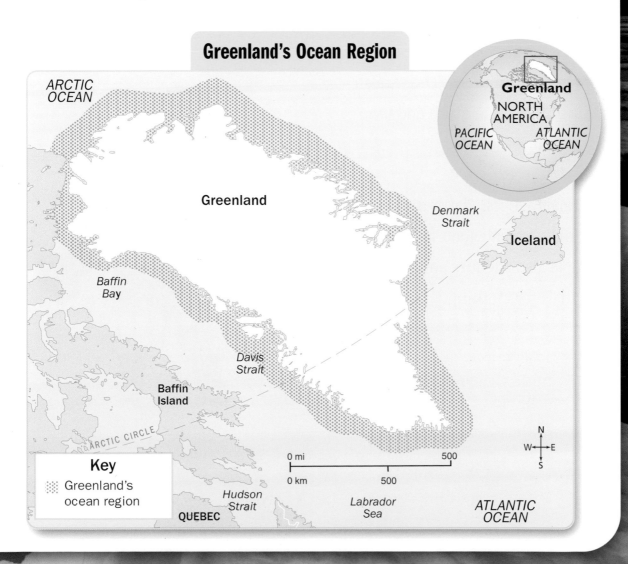

Greenland's Ocean Region

Natural Resources

The ocean provides people with many **natural resources**. Natural resources are things found in nature that people can use. Most of the things that people make, wear, or eat start out as natural resources.

natural resources materials that are found in nature and are useful to people

There are many different kinds of natural resources. Trees, water, metals, and rocks are all examples of natural resources. They are all things found in nature and used by people.

Animals are also natural resources. Animals provide food for people. People also use furs and skins from animals for clothing.

A Greenland boy wearing animal-skin clothing

Resources from Greenland's Ocean Region

Marine animals are natural resources found in Greenland's ocean region. The ocean waters around Greenland have many different kinds of marine animals. This is because the waters are rich in **nutrients**. Nutrients are food for the tiny plants and animals that grow there. Many different fish and other marine creatures stay in the area to feed on these tiny plants and animals.

Many countries send boats to fish in the ocean waters around Greenland. The fish they catch provide food for people around the world.

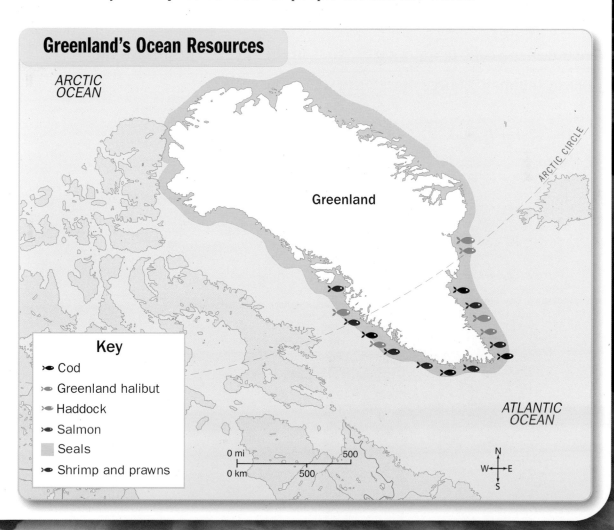

Greenland's Ocean Resources

ARCTIC OCEAN

Greenland

ARCTIC CIRCLE

ATLANTIC OCEAN

Key
- Cod
- Greenland halibut
- Haddock
- Salmon
- Seals
- Shrimp and prawns

0 mi — 500
0 km — 500

N
W — E
S

The Ocean and the Water Cycle

The oceans around Greenland are an important resource. The oceans play a key part in the water cycle. In the water cycle, the sun warms Earth's water. Some of the water then rises into the air as vapor. This vapor forms into clouds. The water returns to Earth as rain that falls from the clouds.

The water cycle is important for Earth. The rain provides water that keeps plants alive. It also provides drinking water for people and animals.

About 97 percent of water on Earth is in the ocean. This makes the ocean the main source of water in the water cycle.

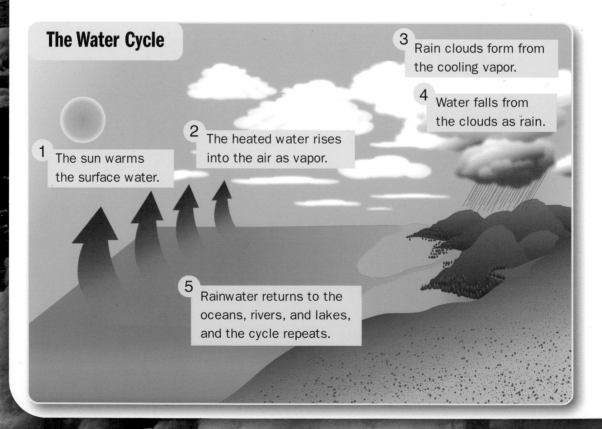

The Water Cycle

1 The sun warms the surface water.

2 The heated water rises into the air as vapor.

3 Rain clouds form from the cooling vapor.

4 Water falls from the clouds as rain.

5 Rainwater returns to the oceans, rivers, and lakes, and the cycle repeats.

How Ocean Resources Are Used

The oceans around Greenland are rich in fish and other seafood.
Fish is the main source of food for the people of Greenland. This
seafood is also sold to other countries. In this way, the people of
Greenland make money.

People in fishing boats catch fish and other seafood in nets or on
lines. The fish are then taken to a harbor. Some of the fish are sold
to local people to eat. The rest of the fish are taken to factories to be
frozen and packaged. This fish is sent to other countries to be sold.

Workers prepare seafood for export at a factory in Greenland.

Food from the Ocean

Fish and other seafood found in the ocean waters around Greenland have special qualities, or **properties**.

Haddock

Fish found in Greenland's ocean waters include Greenland halibut, Norway haddock, salmon, and cod. One property of these fish is that they are rich in vitamins and protein. Greenland halibut, a large, flat fish, is a good source of **vitamin D**. Cod and haddock, which are smaller fish, are high in **protein**.

There are also many shrimp and prawns around Greenland. Shrimp and prawns are small shellfish. Greenland sells shellfish to other countries. One property of shellfish is that they are rich in **iron**.

A fisherman catches a halibut in a Greenland inlet.

Other Products from the Ocean

There are some parts of marine animals that people do not eat. Some of these parts have properties that are useful for other products. Parts such as the livers, stomachs, and shells are used to make food for pets and farm animals. These parts are also sometimes made into fertilizers. Fertilizers are substances added to soil to help plants grow.

In the past, the people of Greenland hunted seals and whales. They hunted these animals for food. They used the skins of seals for clothing. They sold meat and other animal parts to other countries. Today many whales and seals are endangered. The people of Greenland can still hunt these animals, but they must use the animals themselves. They cannot sell the animals outside their country.

Traditional sealskin boots from Greenland

Using Earth's Resources Wisely

The ocean provides people with many useful resources. However, not all resources last forever. There are two kinds of natural resources on Earth. These are **renewable** resources and **nonrenewable** resources. Renewable resources are replaced by nature. Water and animals are examples of renewable resources. Nonrenewable resources take much longer to form. Nonrenewable resources cannot be replaced.

Many of Earth's resources are being used up. Some nonrenewable resources may run out in the near future. People need to take care now to ensure that these resources do not run out.

Renewable Resources		Nonrenewable Resources	
Animals		Metals	
Plants		Gemstones	
Fresh water		Oil	
		Natural gas	
		Coal	

Conservation

Conservation is one way people can help save Earth's resources. Conservation is the careful use of a resource to save it for the future.

conservation
protection and careful use of natural resources

Years of fishing and hunting in Greenland have brought down the numbers of some marine animals. There are now fewer Greenland halibut, salmon, cod, and seals than there used to be.

Laws have now been made to conserve ocean animals. Countries that fish in the waters around Greenland have a limit on how many fish they can catch. The people of Greenland are now only allowed to hunt seals for their own use.

Fishing boats around Greenland, such as this one, now have limits on the number of fish they can catch.

Recycling

Another way people can help save resources is by **recycling**. To recycle is to turn used materials into new products.

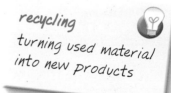

recycling
turning used material into new products

One resource that can be recycled is water. Much of the waste water from homes, farms, and factories ends up in the ocean. This waste water can harm sea animals that need clean water to survive.

Many countries have now set up units that collect unclean water. They put the water through a cleaning process. Then the water can be used again.

Some of the water you use may be recycled.

Think About the Key Concepts

Think about what you read. Think about the maps and diagrams. Use these to answer the questions. Share what you think with others.

1. Name two or more resources from the country you read about in this book.

2. Name at least three ways the natural resources discussed in this book are used.

3. Explain the difference between a renewable resource and a nonrenewable resource.

4. Give at least two examples of how people can conserve Earth's resources.

Resource Map

A resource map shows you the natural resources found in an area.
Resource maps often use symbols to show where the different kinds of resources are found.

Resource maps can show different kinds of resources.
Look back at the resource map on page 9. It shows where the main fishing areas are around Greenland. The map on page 19 is also a resource map. It shows the main fishing areas around the world.

How to Read a Resource Map

1. **Read the title.**
   The title tells you which type of resource will be shown on the map.

2. **Read the key.**
   The key tells you what the different symbols represent.

3. **Study the map.**
   Find the symbols on the map to see which resources are found in which areas.

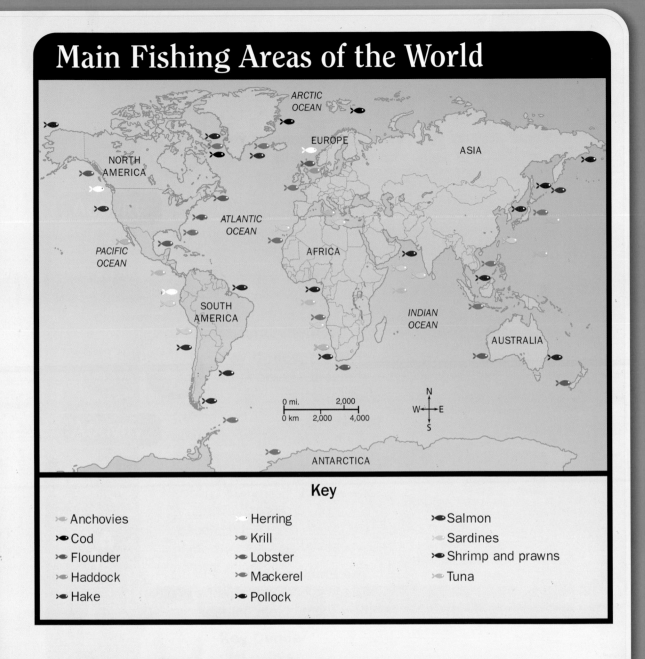

Main Fishing Areas of the World

Key

- Anchovies
- Cod
- Flounder
- Haddock
- Hake
- Herring
- Krill
- Lobster
- Mackerel
- Pollock
- Salmon
- Sardines
- Shrimp and prawns
- Tuna

What's on the Map?

Read the map by following the directions on page 18. Then use the map to answer the following questions. What types of fish are found off the coast of West Africa? What are two coasts where people fish for herring? What kinds of fish are found near where you live?

Problem-Solution Article

A problem-solution article describes a problem and gives possible solutions to the problem. The problem-solution article beginning on page 21 describes the problem of pollution in the waters around Greenland.

A problem-solution article usually contains the following:

The Introduction
The introduction outlines the problem.

The Problem
The first body paragraphs explain how the problem came about.

The Solutions
The next body paragraphs give some possible solutions to the problem.

Saving Greenland's Ocean Region

The **title** tells you the topic of the article.

The ocean region that surrounds Greenland is an important resource. But pollution is a major problem affecting the ocean. Industries across the world dump their wastes into the ocean. Some of this polluted water reaches the Greenland region. It affects the plants, animals, and people who live there.

The **introduction** outlines the problem.

The number of ships in the area has been rising. Fishing ships and ships exploring for oil create many problems for ocean animals. Mining in the area leaves behind many chemicals. These chemicals may be poisonous to animals and people.

Photographs support the facts in the text.

Pollution from shipping is becoming a problem in Greenland.

The Problem: Pollution

There are several causes of the pollution problem in Greenland's ocean region. These include the dumping of industrial chemicals, mining, and oil exploration.

> The first body paragraphs explain how the **problem** came about.

Industrial Chemicals

Waste chemicals from industries are often dumped into the ocean. These chemicals can travel long distances. Some even reach the Arctic region around Greenland. Many of the chemicals are poisonous. The poisons enter plants in the water. The poisons then enter the fish that feed on the plants. Larger animals like whales and seals eat the fish. The poisons are passed from the fish to the larger animals. They build up in the animals' bodies and may kill the animals. The poisons may also affect people who eat the animals.

Mining

In some areas of Greenland, mining is an important industry. The ground in these areas is rich in valuable materials. These include diamonds, gold, silver, copper, tin, lead, and zinc.

Many Greenlanders hunt sea animals for food.

Oil spills can harm animals.

Mining pollutes the ocean waters around Greenland. Waste materials flow into glaciers and water channels. From there they are carried to the ocean. The Maarmorilik lead and zinc mine in northwest Greenland is one mine that has caused pollution. The mine used to release 30 poisonous substances. The poisons killed almost all the seals and Beluga whales in the area. The mine was closed in 1990. But the poisons will remain in the area for many years.

Oil Exploration

Oil exploration has added to the pollution problem. The Arctic region has large amounts of oil beneath its ocean. Companies from different parts of the world explore or drill for oil in the area. However, ships holding the oil can sometimes spill the oil. When spilled oil spreads over the water, it blocks out air and light. The oil coats fish, seabirds, and other ocean animals. Many plants and animals die as a result of a spill.

The Solutions

There are several ways of solving the problem of pollution in Greenland's ocean region. Many countries are working to reduce ocean pollution. People are trying to solve the problem by using safer mining methods. They are also protecting natural areas. An oil spill sensitivity atlas is also useful.

The next body paragraphs give some possible **solutions** to the problem.

Reducing Pollution

Many industries are now trying to help find solutions to the pollution problem. Fifty countries have signed the Stockholm Convention. The convention is a worldwide treaty to prevent and reduce pollutants getting into the environment. By signing the convention, governments agreed to stop using 12 poisonous chemicals and pesticides. They stopped using the chemicals and pesticides in May 2004.

The signing of the Stockholm Convention

Safer Mining

Using safer mining methods is another way of solving the pollution problem. Many mining companies are now making sure that they do not spill their wastes. The National Environmental Research Institute in Greenland carries out studies on mining activities. It studied the environment at the Maarmorilik mine in northwest Greenland. When the mine closed, the area was cleaned to reduce pollution.

Oil Spill Sensitivity Atlas

Greenland has made an oil spill sensitivity atlas. The atlas helps people stop further pollution. The atlas shows areas where oil exploration is taking place. It gives information on ocean resources present in the areas. The atlas can help people reduce the damage of an oil spill if it occurs.

West Greenland

Eqalumniut Nunaat - Nassuttup Nunaa

High
Extreme
Ramsar Area

Sisimiut

High and Extreme Sensitivities

0   100 km

Maniitsoq

Nuuk

Ikkattoq and Western Islands

N
W—E
S

Paamiut

The oil spill sensitivity atlas shows areas where the environment and wildlife would be most affected by an oil spill. The Ramsar areas shown on the map are important wetland areas for water birds as named by the Ramsar Convention on Wetlands.

Protected Areas

The Greenland government has turned the northeastern part of the country into a national park. This is to protect the area from further pollution damage. The Greenland National Park has an area of more than 500,000 square kilometers (193,050 square miles). Icecaps and glaciers cover most of the area. The park protects the marine plants and animals in the area.

People all over the world are being educated about the dangers of polluting the ocean. Protecting the ocean means that its natural resources last forever.

Greenland National Park is a protected area.

Apply the **Key Concepts**

Key Concept 1 Earth provides many natural resources that people can use.

Activity

Write a list of four things that you use every day, such as kinds of food or clothing. Then write down the natural resources that these things come from. For example, they might come from plants or animals.

1. Wool sweater: wool comes from sheep

2. Apples: grow on trees

3.

Key Concept 2 Different resources are useful to people in different ways.

Activity

Create a chart with three columns. In the first column, name some resources found in Greenland's ocean region. In the second column, name the special properties of each natural resource. In the third column, name the ways people use each natural resource.

Resource	Properties	Uses

Key Concept 3 Conservation and recycling can help save resources.

Activity

Write a short letter to a conservation group. Give two reasons why you think Greenland's ocean region should be conserved. Give one suggestion for how people can help conserve the ocean.

To whom it may concern:

RESEARCH AND WRITE

Write Your Own Problem-Solution Article

You have read the problem-solution article about pollution around Greenland. Now you can write your own problem-solution article.

1. Study the Model

Look back at pages 21–26. Read the labels to find the important features of a problem-solution article. What information is presented in the introduction section of the article? What information is presented in *The Problem* section of the article? What information is presented in *The Solutions* section of the article?

2. Choose Your Topic

Now you can choose your topic. Your topic will be a conservation issue. It must involve a problem for which there are possible solutions. You may choose an animal that is at risk of dying out. You may choose an area where the natural environment is at risk. You may already know of a conservation cause that you would like to research. Otherwise, look on the Internet and through books and magazines to get some ideas.

Writing a Problem-Solution Article

◆ Choose a topic related to conservation. The topic must have a problem and possible solutions.

◆ Write an introduction explaining what needs to be conserved.

◆ Write several body paragraphs describing the problem.

◆ Write several more paragraphs giving some solutions to the problem.

3. Research Your Topic

Write down notes on what you already know about your topic. Organize them into columns labeled "Problem" and "Solution." Then think about what else you will need to find out. Remember that you will need to discuss the conservation problem in the first section. In the second section, you will need to present some possible solutions to the problem.

Topic: Giant Pandas

Problem	Solution
Habitat destruction	Protect the bamboo forests

Make a list of questions. Use this list to guide your research. Then look through books and magazines. Go on the Internet. Take notes on what you find out and add them to your chart. Make copies of pictures you may want to use.

4. Write a Draft

Now you can write a draft of your article. Look back at the article on pages 21–26. Use it as a model for writing your article.

5. Revise and Edit

Read your draft. Check to see that it is well organized. Keep your research nearby so you can check that all the facts are correct. Look for any words that are misspelled. Make sure that each sentence starts with a capital letter.

Create a Conservation Poster

Now you can share your work. You can design a poster about your conservation cause. Then you can share your poster with the rest of the class.

How to Make a Poster

1. Think of a slogan.
A slogan is a catchy phrase. It sums up your conservation goal, for example, "Save the Pandas." Write your slogan in big letters on your poster paper.

2. Include a strong photograph or illustration.
Use a copy of a photograph you found during your research. Or draw an illustration on your poster. The photograph or illustration should show the animal or natural environment that you want to conserve.

3. Write some information about the cause.
Write a short paragraph about your animal or natural environment. Tell why it needs to be conserved. Give important facts. For example, you could write the number of pandas alive today compared to 50 years ago. Keep your sentences short and to the point.

4. Share your work.
Hang all the class posters on the classroom wall. As a class, walk around the room and read each other's posters. Be prepared to answer any questions your classmates may have about your conservation cause.

Glossary

conservation – protection and careful use of natural resources

iron – a substance people need to keep their blood and muscles healthy

marine – relating to the ocean

natural resources – materials that are found in nature and are useful to people

nonrenewable – not able to be replaced once it is used

nutrients – substances that help people or animals grow or remain healthy

properties – special features or qualities

protein – a substance people need to help their bodies grow and repair injuries

recycling – turning used material into new products

renewable – able to be replaced by nature once it is used

vitamin D – a substance people need to keep their bones healthy

Index